BRITISH INDEPENDENT BUS AND COACH OPERATORS

A SNAPSHOT FROM THE 1960s

BRITISH INDEPENDENT BUS AND COACH OPERATORS

A SNAPSHOT FROM THE 1960s

JIM BLAKE

PEN & SWORD
TRANSPORT

AN IMPRINT OF PEN & SWORD BOOKS LTD.
YORKSHIRE – PHILADELPHIA

First published in Great Britain in 2020 by
Pen and Sword Transport
An imprint of
Pen & Sword Books Ltd
Yorkshire - Philadelphia

Copyright © Jim Blake, 2020

ISBN 978 1 47385 714 8

Typeset by Aura Technology and Software Services, India.

Printed and bound in India by Replika Press Pvt. Ltd.

Pen & Sword Books Ltd incorporates the Imprints of Pen & Sword Books Archaeology, Atlas, Aviation, Battleground, Discovery, Family History, History, Maritime, Military, Naval, Politics, Railways, Select, Transport, True Crime, Fiction, Frontline Books, Leo Cooper, Praetorian Press, Seaforth Publishing, Wharncliffe and White Owl.

For a complete list of Pen & Sword titles please contact

PEN & SWORD BOOKS LIMITED
47 Church Street, Barnsley, South Yorkshire, S70 2AS, England
E-mail: enquiries@pen-and-sword.co.uk
Website: www.pen-and-sword.co.uk

or

PEN AND SWORD BOOKS
1950 Lawrence Rd, Havertown, PA 19083, USA
E-mail: Uspen-and-sword@casematepublishers.com
Website: www.penandswordbooks.com

CONTENTS

INTRODUCTION

This is the fifth in my series of photographic albums of British buses and coaches in the 1960s, and probably features the most diverse collection of pictures of different types of vehicles of all of them. This is because it deals with independent bus and coach operators.

Independent fleets themselves varied enormously in size and scope of operation, ranging from major operators such as Barton Transport of Chilwell, Nottinghamshire; Lancashire United and West Riding who operated stage carriage services as well as coach fleets; or Wallace Arnold Tours of Leeds who were a major coach touring company in Britain and in Continental Europe, to small operators who possessed just a handful of vehicles. These latter were sometimes involved only in private hire work, for such things as outings to sporting events or theatres, sometimes school or industrial contracts and sometimes a combination of both. Smaller operators were based throughout the country, sometimes in tiny villages and at the other end of the scale, also in the heart of large cities.

It was often the case that smaller operators, particularly those working school contracts or staff buses for industrial concerns, bought up redundant buses and coaches from major operators, whether from BET, BTC (Tilling) or municipal concerns, or indeed my own local operator London Transport. Many got bargains from the latter, in the shape of surplus RT and RTL class double-deckers sold following the disastrous bus strike and service cuts of 1958, in some cases when only four years old. Many of them worked for many years longer with their new operators than they had at home in London, and could be seen throughout Britain. Conversely, redundant buses bought by independent fleets often brought types that came from as far away as Scotland to London and the south east.

In the 1960s, the oldest buses and coaches to be seen with independent fleets were usually those employed on school or industrial contracts. These were not subject to the rigorous testing that governed those carrying fare-paying passengers and therefore could sometimes be kept going until they were literally falling apart! These were known as 'non-PSVs', i.e. non-public service vehicles.

On the other hand, some very small independent fleets, often with the title 'Luxury Coaches', took great pride in their fleets. They would purchase new coaches every two or three years and keep them in immaculate condition.

Generally speaking, the larger fleets – for instance Lancashire United and West Riding – would purchase their vehicles new. However the equally large Barton fleet based in Chilwell, Nottinghamshire was well-known for buying second-hand vehicles from all manner of concerns, as well as buying vehicles new, and the result was a tremendously varied and fascinating fleet.

Another thing which made independent operators so interesting in the 1960s was that some of them merely dumped old buses and coaches at their premises after they had been withdrawn from service. Rather then selling them for scrap, they were cannibalised for spare parts or used as store-sheds. A notable example of this was the Staffordshire independent bus and coach operator Beresford of Cheddleton, who when I visited their depot in June 1967 still had the skeletons of buses dating from the 1920s in their yard!

During the 1960s, I visited many independent bus and coach operators throughout most of England. In addition, I often travelled to Wembley Stadium where buses and coaches of all sorts, shapes and sizes would bring spectators to various sporting events from all over the country. Similarly, coaches and occasionally stage-carriage buses belonging to independent fleets would work as 'reliefs' for major operators' express coach services in the summer to and from Victoria Coach Station, where I spent many summer Saturdays in those days.

The result is that I took very many photographs of the vehicles concerned, concentrating on the older and unusual ones, but also sometimes catching the very latest in bus and coach design. I am therefore pleased to be able to present a selection of them here, few of which have ever been published before. They are presented in chronological order.

May I put on record my thanks to the PSV Circle, from whose news-sheets my original records of most of the vehicles were compiled fifty or so years ago. Also may I thank The Omnibus Society, John Kaye of the Omnibus Touring Circle, Alan Osborne of the Eastern National Enthusiasts Group, and the late George Ledger and Martin Haywood who organised some of the trips to these fleets back in the 'old days' for making many of the pictures possible. Thanks also go to my old friends Paul Everett and Ken Wright, who were often with me in those days, for refreshing my memory on some of the vehicle details, and to Colin Clarke and John Scott-Morgan for making this book possible in the first place.

JIM BLAKE
Palmers Green
August 2020

By the mid-1960s, buses carrying wartime Utility bodywork were very rare indeed, but on 7/9/65, such a vehicle in the shape of Chambers of Bures' Roe-bodied Guy Arab I 55-seater GV9614 is seen in Colchester Bus Station. This was a place where many independent stage-carriage operators' vehicles could be seen at this period. All of this makes the Eastern National Bristol KSW on the right boring by comparison.

Early post-war 29-seat Bedford OBs were also getting scarce by this time, but at Colchester on the same day, this view captures two with the same operator, despite their different liveries. ONO177 is red, whilst ONO711 is blue, but both, which have Duple Vista bodywork, belong to Bennett of Boxted.

Barton of Chilwell was one of the best-known independent stage-carriage operators in the 1960s. On 8/8/65, their 1953 all-Leyland Titan PD2/12 58-seater No.731 is seen at Nottingham's Huntingdon Street bus station. This Titan had been new to the operator which, however, was well-known for its variety of second-hand vehicles too.

Old buses were frequently used by building contractors for staff buses after withdrawal by major operators. An example of this, seen on 8/8/63, is HWO381, an all-Leyland lowbridge 53-seat Titan PD2/1 that had been new to Red & White in 1950. It is seen in Tankerton, Kent near where I was on holiday at the time with my parents, who are seen at the rear of the bus.

Another former major company vehicle used as workmen's transport is KRB87, which had been No.201 in the Midland General fleet and is a 32-seat Saunders-bodied Leyland Tiger PS1 dating from 1948. It now belongs to British Railways, Eastern Region, in whose works yard at Finsbury Park it is seen on 8/2/64, and still carries its previous operator's dark blue and cream livery.

One of the best-known independent operators was Grey Green, based in Stamford Hill, North London not far from my home. On 15/2/64, their Duple Vega Major-bodied Bedford VAL14 448GYR has recently been delivered when seen at the ill-fated Kings Cross, Pentonville Road Coach Station. Independent fleets ran services from here to the north and to East Anglia – as in this case where the coach is bound for Dovercourt, Harwich, Walton and Frinton.

Old buses and coaches were also often bought by fairground showmen, for use as living quarters and/or means of towing their equipment. On 30/3/64, CHU568 is seen at one of the famous Hampstead Heath fairs. This is a Bristol JO5G that had been new to the Bristol Omnibus Company in 1936, and given a new ECW 35-seat body in 1949.

Also at Hampstead Heath that day, EOR579 is a wartime Utility Guy Arab I that had been new to Aldershot & District, and has now been cut down to open-top.

A well-known independent operator was Cambridgeshire-based Premier Travel. An Omnibus Society tour to their Chrishall headquarters on 10/5/64 sees their No.38 (GCE122) out of use. This is a 31-seat Mulliner-bodied Bedford OB dating from the early post-war years.

Bearing blinds that have obviously been set as a joke for the benefit of photographers on the tour, former West Yorkshire Bristol K5G's BWY993 and BWY988, Now No. 119 and 126 in Premier Travel's fleet, date from 1937 but were given new 55-seat lowbridge ECW bodies in 1949.

Two oddities in Premier Travel's varied fleet are No.145 (DCK214), a full-fronted Burlingham-bodied Leyland Titan PD2 which had been new to Ribble, in whose fleet they were nicknamed 'White Ladies', and No.73, a Daimler CVD6 with very rare Wilkes & Meade bodywork which presumably has made its last trip to or from Cambridge!

A really rare survivor seen on 17/5/64, being used as static accommodation at North London's Alexandra Palace fair, is former London Transport forward-entrance Country Area STL1504 (CXX491). One of a batch of fifty built in 1936, it had been withdrawn in 1950. By coincidence, some of this batch had still been in use by London Transport as tree-loppers until just a few months before this picture was taken, but this one was the only one to survive with its upper deck intact. Sadly, it was burnt out by gypsies during the winter of 1964/65 and the remains sold for scrap. However its front registration plate survives: it had fallen off the vehicle when I took this picture, so I 'rescued' it – and still have it today!

Also at Alexandra Palace that day is JG9933, a former East Kent Park Royal-bodied Leyland Tiger TS8 coach new in 1937. It suffered the same fate as the STL above, unfortunately.

Odd man out amongst all the Bristol/ECW double-deckers working for Tilling fleet Southern Vectis on the Isle of Wight is GDL764, an all-Leyland Titan PD2/1 lowbridge 55-seater new in 1950 to Seaview Services. It is seen at Ryde Esplanade in what would be its last season in service on 28/5/64.

Representing some of the more quaint coaches that could be seen on hire to major operators on summer Saturdays at Victoria, KKM131 is a 1949-built 29-seat Duple Vista-bodied Bedford OB with Blue Rambler of Cliftonville, seen approaching Victoria Coach Station on hire to East Kent on 25/7/64.

My summer holiday was again spent in East Kent territory that year. Here on 6/8/64, former Ribble 1951 all-Leyland Royal Tiger PSU1/15 41-seat coach DRN760 is seen in Dover working for Contract Bus Services.

Also working as a building contractor's staff bus, OCN83 is a former Northern General Beadle coach with mechanical parts from a pre-war AEC chassis. It is seen in Brighton on 19/8/64.

Also in Brighton that day, wartime Utility Duple 28-seat Bedford OWB GLH203 is seen dumped on waste ground, having latterly been used as a mobile shop for a greengrocer!

A much older vehicle still very much in service is Gosport & Fareham ('Provincial') 1936 Park Royal-bodied AEC Regent I 56-seater No.45. It was new to this operator, which was renowned for its elderly and unusual vehicles, and is seen at Gosport Ferry on 26/8/64.

At the same location, two of Provincial's more unusual buses are No.73, a wartime Guy Arab I double-decker given a new Reading full-fronted 56-seat body in 1961, and No. 75, an AEC Regal 4 new in 1934, which has a full-fronted 34-seat body new in 1958.

The three vehicles seen above make Provincial No.62 seem new! This is a recently-acquired ex-Southampton Corporation Guy Arab III, new in 1948 with Park Royal 56-seat bodywork.

A strange spectacle at the Kings Cross, Pentonville Road coach station on 8/10/64 is that of these three Barton 1948 Duple 39-seat Leyland Tiger PS1/1s. Nos 557, 566 and 567 are the last survivors of their batch and for some reason have their seats removed and are carrying bicycles!

Bere Regis & District was a well-known independent operator in south-west England. Here on 11/10/64, their 534JBU, a new Plaxton 'Panorama' 51-seat Leyland Leopard coach, is seen parked at the coach park in London's Waterloo Road, perhaps having brought a sightseeing party to town.

Cronshaw of
Hendon was a
well-known London
coach operator.
Here, LBV301, a
Leyland Tiger Cub
PSUC1/2 with Duple
'Britannia' 41-seat
bodywork new in
1959, is one of many
coaches that have
brought spectators
to Sir Winston
Churchill's state
funeral on 30/1/65,
and is parked at
Smithfield.

A remarkable
old vehicle seen
in Victoria Street,
Westminster on
20/2/65 is JA5514, a
1936 Leyland Tiger
TS6, still with its
original Harrington
32-seat bodywork!
This coach had
been new to the
North Western Road
Car Company of
Stockport, who sold
it in 1953 to Gilbert's
Coaches of Tunbridge
Wells, for whom it is
still operating here.
Others of its batch
were rebodied after
the war, therefore
making this one with
its original coachwork
very rare indeed.

Gilbert's were well-known for keeping older coaches in service. Another seen the same day outside Westminster Central Hall is their 1947 Duple Vista 29-seat Bedford OB BJR679 – actually one of their **newer** coaches!

Another use for retired buses in the mid-1960s was as transport for beat groups doing 'one-night-stands' up and down the country. On 26/2/65, former Midland General 1946 Duple-bodied AEC Regal I 35-seater JRB130 is seen parked at Waterloo while performing this function for Pye group, The Beatmen, who as far as I am aware did **not** record for the legendary Holloway Road record producer Joe Meek.

Typifying some of the very unusual coaches still to be seen in the mid-1960s, LLT367 is a Foden with full-fronted Duple 37-seat coachwork, new in 1951. It is seen in Dartford in the ownership of Arnold, East Peckham (Kent) on 27/2/65.

Dating from 1949 and of more conventional design, though by now a type becoming rare, JXC778 is a Dennis Lancet J3 with Duple 35-seat coachwork. Belonging to Parco of Gosport, it appears to have been abandoned in Rosebery Avenue, Holborn.

Midland Road, running between St Pancras Station and the former Midland Railway Somers Town Goods depot, was a favourite place for coaches bringing people to London's theatres or sporting events to park up. On 10/4/65, 1955 Duple-bodied AEC Reliance 41-seater SWA234 is parked there. New to Sheffield United Tours, it is now operated by East Anglian independent operator Soham & District.

On the same day, this very rare Whitson-bodied Crossley SD42/7 33-seat coach, GDL33, is parked at Lincoln's Inn Fields, Holborn. New as No.103 in 1949 to Isle of Wight Tilling Group fleet Southern Vectis, it is now an ambulance for the Walthamstow Handicapped People's Association. Note how it still carries its Southern Vectis fleet number below its windscreen.

Early post-war
Gurney Nutting-bodied Leyland Tiger PS2 35-seater coach DTK345 is seen in Waterloo Road coach park on 6/4/65. It had been new to Bere Regis & District, but is now operated by Johnston of Marnhill. It too is now a rarity.

Brand new, but itself a great rarity even then, LMP721C is a Bedford J3LZ with Realle Grosvenor 21-seat bodywork in the fleet of Monico Coaches of Kentish Town. It stands outside Westminster Abbey on 16/4/65.

Seen on 24/4/65 in The Strand with a London Transport RTW following on route 11, PAE596 is a very rare coach indeed. It is a Beadle-Sentinel integral vehicle, belonging to Bugler Coaches of Bristol.

Also a rarity, 239HUM is an Albion Victor with Duple Firefly coachwork, one of two supplied to Wallace Arnold of Leeds in 1964. It is at Wembley for the FA Cup Final on 1/5/65, at which Liverpool beat Leeds United 2-1.

At Kings Cross Coach Station the following week on 8/5/65, brand new Yelloway Harrington Legionnaire-bodied Bedford VAL14 51-seater CDK411C is in London for the Rugby League Cup Final, at which Hunslet played Wigan.

Arriving at Wembley for the same event is Samuel Ledgard of Leeds' UUA791, a 1955 AEC Reliance with Burlingham 'Seagull' 41-seat coachwork. This operator was well-known for its stage carriage operation in the Leeds and Bradford areas.

A vehicle that has not had so far to travel to the event is former London Transport RT1409 (JXC172), one of the 120 non-standard Cravens-bodied examples built in 1949 and sold in 1956/57. Initially operated after sale by Garelochhead Bus Services in Scotland, it passed to Lewington's Clintona Coaches of Harold Wood early in 1964 and is still with them here. Withdrawn a few months later, it languished in a dealer's yard until the early 1980s when it was acquired for spare parts by the Woolwich Transport Museum. Most ironically, its engine ended up in a preserved standard RT (RT2629) with which I was involved at the time.

Still in London on Sunday 9/5/65, the day after the match, Jackson of Chorley's 1952 Duple-bodied Bedford SB 33-seater coach VMV963 is parked in Midland Road. It was common practice for people coming to see matches at Wembley (or elsewhere in London) to come down from the north of England and spend the night at London hotels afterwards, and perhaps also visit cinemas or theatres as part of their weekend outing. This Duple-bodied Bedford is typical of the first examples of this successful type, which followed the OBs into production in the early 1950s.

More common, of course, with independent operators were ex-London RTs with standard Park Royal or Weymann bodies. One of these, seen at Waterloo Road on 20/5/65, is former RT191 (HLW178) with Knightswood Coaches of Watford. Sold by LT in 1958, this RT is now immaculately preserved in original London Transport condition.

One of the varied fleet of Nottinghamshire independent Barton of Chilwell, their No.711 is a Barton BTS1/1 with Plaxton 37-seat full-fronted bodywork new in 1953, but in fact containing mechanical parts of pre-war Leyland Lion vehicles on chassis reconstructed by the operator themselves. It is seen on Victoria Embankment on 22/5/65.

Essex County
Coaches of Stratford was a well-known East London tour operator, who had a number of AEC Reliances with Roe coachwork, which was unusual for fleets in the London area. Also on 22/5/65, one of these, MJD762, a 37-seater dating from 1959, has arrived at Kings Cross Coach Station and is by now the last survivor of its type in the fleet.

Just as important as ex-company buses and coaches used by independent operators as school buses were those actually owned by local authorities for the purpose. One such is MUL608, one of many Dennis Tritons that were once part of the London County Council's fleet of school buses. Built in 1951 and seen at Tower Hill on 23/5/65, it is now the very last survivor of its type, having passed to the Inner London Education Authority on 1 April when, essentially, the old LCC and Middlesex County Council were combined to form the new Greater London Council.

Also at Kings Cross Coach Station, which was by now threatened with closure, SUG20 is a 1954 Leyland Tiger Cub with Burlingham Seagull 41-seat coachwork which had been new to Wallace Arnold. By now, however, on 29/5/65, its owner is Dack's Coaches of Terrington.

Seen in the shadow of my place of employment, County Hall, on the same day is XKT781, a genuinely unique vehicle. With a Commer 25A chassis, it carries the only Beadle 'Canterbury' coach body ever built, seating 29 and originally a demonstrator for its builder, Beadle of Rochester, in 1958. It is seen here with Clevedon Motorways of Somerset.

Seen on waste ground in Brighton on 30/5/65, SXD598 is a 1956 Bedford SBG with 36-seat coachwork by Thurgood of Ware. Originally built for London coach tours operator Evan Evans (ETE), it is now in non-PSV use with a contractor. Thurgood bodies were by now quite rare.

Apparently dumped out of use at the same location is PPJ450, another Bedford SB with rare coachwork – this time by Gurney-Nutting.

An oddity seen outside Victoria Station on 5/6/65 is FMV837B, a Bedford VAS2 with Duple Midland bodywork built for carrying disabled people. Of note is the fact that its body is obviously wider than its chassis; and also visible is a tail-lift at the rear for loading wheelchairs. Still in the livery of the former Middlesex County Council, it has presumably passed to one of the London boroughs' welfare departments following the MCC's abolition on 1 April.

A trip to Oxford on 9/6/65 finds Worth of Enstone's 1956 61-seat Massey-bodied AEC Regent V SVD676 working to its home town in the city's bus station.

Another independent double-decker seen in Oxford Bus Station that day is Charlton-on-Otmoor Services' LUC104, former London Transport RT3945 which they had bought in March 1964.

A regular operator at Kings Cross Coach Station was Jennings of Clare, Suffolk. On 11/6/65, their 1949 Duple Vista-bodied Bedford OB 29-seater MUM276 was still going strong and in very smart condition.

Not far away, next day 12/6/65, Horseshoe Coaches of Tottenham's SMU36 turns from Midland Road into Euston Road. This fleet, which I well remember being used to take me to football or cricket from my school in Highbury to our playing fields in Walthamstow in the late 1950s and early 1960s, favoured Dennis Lancets. But by now, this one is the only survivor. It has rare Gurney-Nutting 37-seat full-fronted coachwork, and dates from 1949.

A very unusual vehicle to turn up at Victoria Coach Station the same day is Osborne of Tollesbury, Essex, 8071ML. Built in 1962, this was originally an AEC Renown demonstrator with Park Royal 72-seat forward-entrance bodywork. It became well-known as London Transport's RX1 when tried out in their Country Area in 1963 and was later preserved in that guise.

An unusual coach seen parked on Victoria Embankment, with the Houses of Parliament in the background, also on 12/6/65, is NKR250, a 1951 Bedford SB with Thurgood 37-seat coachwork. It belongs to Moody's Coaches of Northfleet, Kent.

Seen in Waterloo Road coach park on 19/6/65, REL792 is an Albion Victor with full-fronted Harrington 37-seat coachwork, built as late as 1955 for Charlie's Cars of Bournemouth and now operating for Parco Coaches of Gosport.

LYM459 has rare Windover coachwork, and is an AEC Regal IV that was new to Timpson's of Catford in 1951. By 26/6/65, when it is seen arriving at Victoria Coach Station on hire to Royal Blue, it belongs to Wessex Coaches.

Also arriving at Victoria Coach Station on 26/6/65, coach UHX711 is not the fairly modern Plaxton-bodied AEC it seems. It was new in 1949, an AEC Regal III originally with a rare Santus body, but upon acquisition several years later by operator Osmond's Coaches of Curry Rivel, was rebodied as seen here. However this Plaxton full-fronted 30-seat body was itself second-hand, having been built to rebody a Maudslay Marathon III coach in 1955! It is seen here on hire to Royal Blue, having worked an Associated Motorways service from the West Country.

Seen outside the premises of Horlock's Coaches, Northfleet on 27/6/65, OTB400 is a Leyland Royal Tiger with extremely rare Beccols 41-seat coachwork, new in 1951.

In the same operator's yard, CEU633 is a 1956 AEC Reliance with Roe 41-seat coachwork.

Fairly modern
Plaxton coachwork again disguises this coach's true origins. MXB555 is a Dennis Lancet J3 new to London operator Glenton Tours in 1952, and rebodied with this full-fronted 30-seat body later in the 1950s. It is seen at the premises of Thatched House Coaches, Barking also on 27/6/65.

Another AEC
Regal III with more recent, full-fronted Plaxton coachwork is CCB353, dating from 1948 and recently acquired by Da Costa Coaches of Holloway, London N7 when seen in Belvedere Road, Waterloo on 28/6/65.

Seen parked off Victoria Street on 3/7/65, JTX563 is a rare Commer Avenger I with Duple 33-seat bodywork, new in 1951. Its operator is Silver Queen Coaches of Worthing.

Loading up at Kings Cross Coach Station for an evening trip to its home town of Clare, Jennings SPU985 is an MCCW-bodied Leyland Olympic 40-seater new in 1950. This type of Leyland underfloor-engined chassis was one of the first of its type, yet quite rare in the UK as many of them were built for the export market. The 15-year-old bus has just been overhauled when seen here.

KOC233 is another Leyland Olympic with Jennings, seen on 10/7/65 also at Kings Cross. It has MCCW 44-seat bodywork, having been new to them as a demonstrator in 1949, so is therefore one of the very first British underfloor-engined single-deckers to be built after the war.

On 18/7/65, I attended an Omnibus Society visit to operators in Suffolk and northern Essex. Our mode of transport was Grey Green 1963 Harrington 'Cavalier'-bodied AEC Reliance 51-seater 422EYO, which is seen upon our arrival in Ipswich. These vehicles were usually used on the operator's coastal express services between London and East Anglia.

Another operator we visited that day was Hedingham & District, which was well-known for acquiring larger operators' vehicles for further service. One such seen at Halstead is their L24 (LHT909), a 1946 Bristol L5G with ECW 35-seat forward-entrance bodywork acquired from the Bristol Omnibus Company. For some reason it was withdrawn and scrapped just a week after this picture was taken.

Premier Travel's independent fleet operated in this area too. Also at Halstead, their No.173 is the last of the twenty-five RF class MCCW-bodied AEC Regal IVs built for London Transport for private hire and touring work in 1951. Premier Travel had acquired seven others of this type early in 1964 immediately following their withdrawal from such duties, but this one (former RF25) had been one of ten converted for Green Line coach duties in 1956, and had been sold earlier. It operated for Super Coaches of Upminster and Peter's Coaches of Hockley before being acquired by Premier Travel. This operator also acquired some standard Green Line RFs that became redundant in the mid-1960s. Former private hire and touring RFs like this one were distinguishable from standard ones by having 'sun roofs' (extra windows above those on the sides) and also by being only 27ft 6ins long rather than the usual 30ft, and seating 35 rather than 39 or 41.

An oddity seen at Waterloo on 19/7/65 is early post-war Thurgood-bodied Albion Victor 35-seat coach LNK22. It looks very striking in the blue and yellow livery of Dye's Coaches of Hertford, to whom it was new, and is a very rare vehicle indeed.

Back on holiday again at Swalecliffe, Kent, I visited nearby Herne Bay where I found CJG990, a 1948 Dennis Lancet J3 with Park Royal bodywork owned by the Herne Bay Old People's Society. This had been new to local BET operator East Kent, and had until recently worked local services between Seasalter, Whitstable, Tankerton, Swalecliffe and Herne Bay where it had been based.

Seen in Canterbury on 28/7/65, AEF654C is a brand new Plaxton Panorama-bodied AEC Reliance touring the area owned by Bee Line Coaches of West Hartlepool. It is accompanied by a Duple 'Super Vega'-bodied Bedford SB dating from a few years earlier in the 1960s. These two typify the modern coaches to be seen around Britain in the mid-1960s.

BET operator East Kent provided most rural and inter-urban bus services in the area after which it was named. However, there were a number of small independent operators working stage carriage services in the area, as shown by Drew of Canterbury's new Duple Midland-bodied Bedford SB5 42-seater EPM153C. It is seen in Canterbury Bus Station.

Banfield's Coaches was a well-known South London independent coach operator that operated coastal express services, private hires and school or industrial contracts and was based at the former London Transport bus garage at Nunhead. On 29/7/65, their 1954 Burlingham Seagull-bodied Leyland Tiger Cub 41-seater 134BMH has apparently broken down on the A299 Thanet Way near Chestfield & Swalecliffe Station!

Another well-known South London coach operator was United. On 1/8/65, their 1955 Duple Vega-bodied Bedford SBO 30-seater RLM591 has worked to Whitstable and Herne Bay. It is parked up at the latter. This coach was a typical member of their fleet fifty-five years ago.

An unusual coach still with a fairly large London coach operator is OXT24, a Duple-bodied Sentinel with Lewis of Greenwich. Dating from 1954, it is parked near Victoria Station on 7/8/65.

A trip to Nottingham on 8/8/65 finds one of Barton of Chilwell's distinctive Duple-bodied Leyland Titan PD1 lowbridge forward-entrance 55-seaters, No.513, at Huntingdon Street Bus Station. This was one of the second batch of these buses, built in 1948.

Another independent operator serving this bus station was Gash of Newark, whose No.2 (KAL579) is a Daimler CVD6 also built in 1948, but given a new Massey 61-seat highbridge body in 1958 and one of a batch of four so treated.

A third independent stage carriage operator serving Nottingham's Huntingdon Street Bus Station was South Notts of Gotham, whose No.70 (670BNN), one of two Leyland Titan PD3/3s with Weymann 67-seat lowbridge bodywork delivered to them in 1958, awaits departure for its home town.

I travelled on South Notts' No.70 to visit their depot at Gotham, where their No.50 (NAL159) is seen. This is one of five all-Leyland PD2/12s with 53-seat bodywork supplied to South Notts between 1951 and 1953. In the background of this view may be seen a number of withdrawn vehicles retained at the depot, some of which will be seen later.

Also at South Notts' depot, No.71 (MVD627) is another Leyland Titan PD2/12, but with NCME 55-seat lowbridge bodywork. New in 1955, it was acquired from Irvin of Salsburgh in 1960. The red double-decker on the right is a Burlingham-bodied Leyland Titan PD2 that had been acquired from Ribble for spare parts only.

South Notts' No.42 (MAL310) is a Leyland Royal Tiger PSU1/15 with Duple 'Roadmaster' 45-seat dual-purpose coachwork seen at their depot too on 8/8/65.

Amongst a row of withdrawn vehicles at the depot of South Notts, Gotham on 8/8/65 are their No.68 (LRR655), a 1950 Duple Vista-bodied Bedford OB 29-seater acquired from Barton of Chilwell, and No.41 (LNN319), a Duple-bodied Leyland Tiger PS1 35-seater new in 1948. The much older vehicle to their left, which unfortunately was obscured from full view, is No.17 (VO8846) a Leyland-bodied Lion 34-seater dating from as long ago as 1935!

Another withdrawn Leyland at South Notts' premises is JP4701, a Leyland-bodied Titan TD7 with 53-seat lowbridge bodywork that had been new to Wigan Corporation. It had an 'unfrozen' chassis, meaning that it was being built when the exigencies of war stopped normal production in 1942, which was released for bodying only when the War Cabinet allowed it to be.

From the late 1950s onwards, Ford began to produce Thames Trader chassis for coaches to compete with Bedford. These carried similar coachwork by such builders as Duple and Plaxton to those supplied for Bedfords, as seen by 716COM, a Trader with a Duple Super Vega 41-seat body built in 1961, and owned by Birmingham operator Allenways, at whose depot it is seen on 29/8/65.

Also at Allenways' depot that day is early post-war Burlingham-bodied Leyland Tiger PS2 35-seat coach LFD554, in the livery of Welsh operator Hills of Tredegar, but apparently now no longer in use.

Another early post-war coach seen next day, Bank Holiday Monday 30/8/65, in Southend's Kursaal coach park is KKK836. This was originally Maidstone & District CO97, one of a large batch of AEC Regal IIIs with unusual Harrington full-fronted 32-seat coachwork supplied between 1946 and 1949. In common with the Duple-bodied Bedford OB on the left, it is now owned by Bluebird Coaches of Ipswich.

At this period, a lot of interesting independent bus and coach operators existed in the Colchester area. One was Vines Coaches of Great Bromley, at whose depot on 7/9/65 is seen MPU395, a Dennis Lancet J3 new in 1947 to Thorpe's Coaches of Dagenham and given a new full-fronted Burlingham Seagull 35-seat body in 1955.

Another elderly vehicle at Vines' depot which will certainly never run again is MTW796, a 1946 AEC Regal I with its original Thurgood half-cab 35-seat body. It is dumped alongside a Windover-bodied Regal IV that had come from Sheffield United Tours.

Another of the independent fleets was Blackwell of Earl's Colne, whose EUH961 is seen the same day in Colchester Bus Station. This is an all-Leyland Titan PD2/3 lowbridge 53-seater, one of two built in 1950 acquired from Western Welsh. Some of the other independent operators' vehicles are seen in the background – the RT is not a former London Transport vehicle, but one of those that had been new to St Helen's Corporation now with Norfolk's of Nayland.

At the depot of Norfolk's of Nayland, CGV70 is a splendid 'old' Dennis Lancet J3, with Thurgood 35-seat coachwork which however dates only from 1950. Lurking in the shadows behind it, CCF574 is a very rare Austin CXB coach of similar vintage.

Another Thurgood-bodied coach with Norfolk's is AGV653, a 29-seat Bedford OB dating from 1948.

Also belonging to an Essex independent fleet, 576FVW is a Commer Avenger III with Duple 41-seat coachwork new in 1956. Seen at Horseguards Avenue, Westminster on 18/9/65, it is with Wicks of Braintree who have recently acquired it from Tilling Group operator Eastern National. It had, however, been new to Moore's of Kelvedon, whose fleet and operations were taken over by Eastern National early in 1963.

A very unusual vehicle seen in Eastbourne on 26/9/65 is LCR214, a full-fronted Albion coach operated by Eastbourne Coachways.

Typifying Barton of Chilwell's fascinating fleet, MAL389 had been their No.633, a Barton BTS1 reconstruction using parts from pre-war Leyland Lions with Strachan dual-purpose 43-seat bodywork new in 1950. Seen at their Chilwell headquarters on 3/10/65 it is now withdrawn and in use as a seat store.

A more drastic conversion of one of Barton's BTS's is that of former No.654 (MVO85) to a fuel tanker! Originally with 43-seat dual-purpose bodywork built by Barton themselves in 1952, it too is now out of use at Chilwell.

In complete contrast to the previous two vehicles, MCCW-bodied Daimler Fleetline 72-seater 7000HP is on loan to Barton. This demonstrator was new in 1962 and delivered in the full livery of Birmingham City Transport, for whom it first ran.

A well-known Hampshire independent operator was King Alfred of Winchester. On 9/10/65, their 1952 all-Leyland Titan PD2/10 lowbridge 55-seater KOR382 is seen in the city centre.

Another stage-carriage operator who ran into Winchester at this period was Porter of Dummer, whose 1950 Duple Vista-bodied Bedford OB 29-seater GDL489 is seen here.

These next three photographs are taken in the last days of the Kings Cross Pentonville Road Coach Station, which was served entirely by independent bus and coach operators. This view taken on 16/10/65 shows B.K. Jennings of Clare's 1957 Duple-bodied AEC Reliance 41-seater 936GMH, which had previously been owned by Banfield Coaches' subsidiary Empire's Best Coaches.

Two more Duple-bodied AEC Reliances at Kings Cross that day are 6801HK, a 41-seater new to Sutton's of Clacton in 1958, and WLY498, a 43-seater new in 1959 that they had acquired from Valliant Coaches of Ealing.

Yet another AEC Reliance at Kings Cross that evening is Yelloway of Rochdale's new Harrington Cavalier 45-seater CDK856C, working their motorway express service to and from Blackpool. Passenger facilities at this coach station were very basic, but after its closure, coaches were initially forced to load and unload their passengers in nearby main roads Pancras Road and York Way where there were no facilities at all. However since both were adjacent to main line railway stations St Pancras and Kings Cross respectively, perhaps passengers' needs could be met there!

Smith's of Reading, Berkshire was a large independent coach operator whose vehicles ran coastal expresses and did private hire and tours work, as well as schools and industrial contracts. On 17/10/65, 1950 Duple Vista-bodied Bedford OB 29-seater URE216 is seen at their depot. It had been acquired from Greatorex of Stafford in 1952.

Various contractors' buses and coaches were also housed and maintained at Smith's depot. An extremely odd vehicle to be seen there the same day is UHR741, a wartime Utility Mulliner-bodied Bedford OWB 28-seater belonging to Chivers of Devizes. The reason it has a 1950s registration is that it had previously belonged to the War Department and therefore had an army or air force registration.

Another oddity at Smith's is their own KJH900, a 1950 Dennis Lancet J3 with Duple 35-seat coachwork. By now, it is used to tow preserved trolleybuses stored at Smith's depot, notably having towed London Transport trolleybus No.260 to and from Reading when it toured the Corporation's system in October 1967!

Also at Smith's depot that day is 1953 Duple Vega-bodied Bedford SB 37-seater PAE766, which appears to have come to grief in an accident and is being stripped for spare parts.

A last look at Kings Cross Pentonville Road Coach Station on 19/10/65: Premier Travel 1955 Burlingham Seagull-bodied AEC Reliance 41-seater No.152 (UAF281) is working their limited stop service 38 to Haverhill and Saffron Waldon.

A strange vehicle seen at Waterloo Road coach park on 24/11/65 is GCT181, a Sentinel STC6 with Sentinel 44-seat bus bodywork dating from the early 1950s. Last operated by Roy's of Kenilworth, it is now in missionary service with the Salvation Army.

On a gloomy 16/12/65, two of Grey Green's older coaches are seen outside their Stamford Hill depot. They have been reinstated for use on the London Transport Northern City Line replacement service between Finsbury Park and Drayton Park, following the curtailment of the branch at the latter point in October 1964 to facilitate building of the new Victoria Line. Both dating from 1960, YLF362 is a Bedford SB8 with Harrington 'Crusader' 37-seat coachwork, whilst YXA372 is also an SB8 but with Duple 'Vega' 41-seat bodywork. The latter is in the livery of subsidiary fleet Fallowfield & Britten.

Actually working the rail replacement service on 8/1/66, Crusader-bodied SB8 YLF361 sets down its few passengers in Bryantwood Road, Drayton Park. When the Victoria Line opened on 1 September 1968 (running non-stop from Highbury & Islington to Finsbury Park), this service was withdrawn, and anyone wanting to travel between Drayton Park and Finsbury Park had to do so by doubling back via Highbury! Only when the BR Eastern Region Great Northern electric service took over the former Northern City Line in the autumn of 1976 was this rail link restored.

A stranger at the Waterloo Road coach park on 29/1/66 is UDE111, a 1954 Plaxton-bodied AEC Reliance 41-seater belonging to Welsh independent operator Silcox of Pembroke Dock.

The Wembley finals season is here again as a hockey match brings the coaches there on 12/3/66. Elderly 1948 Duple 'Vista'-bodied Bedford OB 29-seater FHO595, now operating for Tombs and Drake of Totton contrasts with a more recent Wilts & Dorset Duple 'Bella Vega'-bodied Bedford SB.

For the same event, Boughton's Coaches of Forest Gate, London E7 have sent their 1951 Plaxton-bodied AEC Regal IV HD9675. A typical Tilling Group Bristol/ECW coach follows.

On 26/3/66, I travelled on an Omnibus Society tour visiting operators in the Newbury and Andover area. One of these was the Berkshire independent Reliance of Newbury, at whose depot is seen their No.81 (HXB457), a 1946 Duple-bodied AEC Regal III 35-seater which they acquired in 1962.

Another elderly coach at Reliance's depot is No.23 (ERX284), a Bedford OB with Duple Vista 29-seat coachwork which they bought new in 1948.

Two other second-hand vehicles at Reliance's depot are No.85 (MWL972), a Weymann-bodied AEC Regent III 56-seater new to City of Oxford Motor Services in 1948 and acquired via Smith's of Reading in 1963, and No.107 (REL54), a Duple Vega-bodied Bedford SBO 38-seat coach acquired from Shamrock & Rambler of Bournemouth in 1965.

Dumped at the rear of Reliance's depot are the remains of OEL932, a 1954 Duple-bodied Bedford SBO also acquired from Shamrock & Rambler, but for spare parts only following its involvement in a serious collision.

The coach we travelled on for this trip was almost itself involved in a serious collision when it narrowly avoided a head-on crash with a van coming the other way in a country lane near Newbury. Luckily, the two vehicles just clipped each other, and here members of our party inspect the minor damage. The vehicle is MTW821C, a Ford R192 demonstrator with Duple 'Empress' 45-seat bodywork, which was new in 1965.

In a murky Newbury Bus Station, Reliance No.82 (SX8902) is one of two 1954 Bedford SBOs with Duple Midland 40-seat bus bodies seen working local bus services. This was one of two new to Scottish Oils of Uphill and acquired by Reliance In 1962.

An oddity seen the same day in Newbury is GJT29, an all-Leyland 41-seat Royal Tiger coach dating from the early 1950s and belonging to the Swanage-based Warwickshire Miners' Convalescent Home. Coaches of this type were more usually supplied to major BET fleets such as Maidstone & District, Ribble and Southdown.

Typifying old buses used as workmen's transport by building contractors, KAL132 is an ex-East Midland Weymann-bodied AEC Regal I new in 1946. Now with Eagre Construction, it has broken down on the North Circular Road near Stonebridge Park on 16/4/66.

Seen at Wembley for the Schoolboys' International football final on 30/4/66, LUF608 is a former Southdown Duple-bodied Leyland Royal Tiger new in 1951, and now owned by Churchbridge Coaches of Cannock, Staffordshire.

Also at Wembley that day, JJD400 is a Yeates-bodied AEC Reliance 41-seater coach that has now seen ten years' service with the London Co-operative Society's coaching fleet.

Illustrating how some small independent stage carriage operators bought new double-deckers, DEB484C is a brand new Daimler Fleetline with 76-seat Willowbrook bodywork owned by Burwell & District of Cambridgeshire. Has it really got a standing load of schoolboys on its lower deck?

An older double-decker at Wembley that day is HWN909, a 1952 Weymann-bodied AEC Regent III new to South Wales Transport, and recently acquired by Dickson of Stoke Mandeville.

An unusual little coach parked at Victoria's select Eccleston Square on 7/5/66 is 982LNN, a 14-seat Plaxton-bodied Austin new in 1958 and owned by Wright of Newark.

Back at Wembley on 14/5/66, 864KNU is a Roe-bodied dual-purpose AEC Reliance new in 1959 to South Yorkshire independent Booth & Fisher of Halfway. It is there for the 1966 FA Cup Final in which Everton beat Sheffield Wednesday 3-2, no doubt to the dismay of this coach's passengers!

Next day, 15/5/66, Grey Green 1962 Duple Super Vega-bodied Bedford SB8 41-seater 417ELE is working a railway replacement service for the North London Line when seen outside Broad Street station. It is still in their subsidiary Fallowfield & Britten's maroon and grey livery.

Belle Coaches of Lowestoft, who also used the trading name Classic Coaches as on this vehicle, WBJ637, were well-known for building their own coachwork. That explains this vehicle's unusual appearance! It is a Bedford SBG seating 41 dating from 1955, and is seen at their depot.

Out of action at the depot, KBJ899 is even odder, being an early post-war Maudslay Marathon III with full-fronted 'home-made' coachwork.

305GBJ, a 1957 Belle-bodied Bedford SBG 41-seater accompanies OBJ728, also built by the company, and a 1951 Bedford SB. This however has lost its cab area and engine and is in use as a store! By coincidence, this operator's premises were close to those of a much more famous coachbuilder – Eastern Coachworks (ECW).

In marked contrast to the odd vehicles seen above, FNT225D is a brand new petrol-engined Bedford VAM3 with Duple Empress 45-seat bodywork belonging to Salopia Coaches of Whitchurch. It is at Wembley on 21/5/66 for the Rugby League Cup Final in which St Helen's beat Wigan.

Also at Wembley that day is No.371 of Yorkshire independent operator Hanson's, a Plaxton-bodied Thames Trader coach new in 1962.

Amongst a large contingent of Leeds-based Wallace Arnold's coaches at the event, 8322U is a Plaxton-bodied AEC Reliance built in 1958, and now in its last season of service for this operator.

On a very wet and windswept Epsom Downs for the 1966 Derby on 25/5/66, EFN577 is a former East Kent Dennis Lancet J3 with Duple 32-seat coachwork. Now owned by Herne Bay Old People's Association, it was built only in 1950 despite its pre-war appearance.

Few independent stage carriage operators ran within London Transport's operating area, even in far-flung Country Area towns. One exception, however, was Rover Bus Services of Chesham, Bucks, whose 1954 Duple Midland-bodied Bedford SBO 40-seater UBH697 is seen in Hemel Hempstead Bus Station on 4/6/66.

A better-known Buckinghamshire independent stage carriage operator was Red Rover of Aylesbury, whose buses 'rubbed shoulders' with London Transport's in their home town. This is where, also on 4/6/66, we see their 1963 Park Royal-bodied AEC Bridgemaster 76-seater 6116BH, which they had bought new.

Several other Red Rover buses were former London Transport ones, bearing a red livery just a shade darker than that of LT's Central Area buses. Their RR9 (HLW175) is former RT188, which had been withdrawn by LT in January 1963 and acquired by Keith's Coaches of Aylesbury, the proprietor of the Red Rover fleet, nine months later. It served them until September 1968.

This view at Red Rover's depot, purely by chance and not posed, shows one each of ex-London Transport classes RTL, RTW and RT together. Nearest the camera is former RTL358 (KGU434), with RTW124 (KGK624) in the middle and RT1775 (KYY613) on the left. The latter had also been withdrawn in London in January 1963, but was not acquired by Red Rover until July 1964. It was withdrawn by them four years later. The RTL had been withdrawn as a result of LT's November 1958 service cuts, acquired by Red Rover in July 1959 and eventually withdrawn in January 1973, later to be preserved. The RTW had only been acquired by Red Rover in March 1965, and lasted with them until November 1970.

A smaller independent fleet who had ex-London Transport vehicles was Seth Coaches of Kentish Town, London NW5. These were kept in a nondescript yard just off Kentish Town Road, a peep into which on 5/6/66 reveals two RTs and a GS-class ECW-bodied Guy Special 26-seat single-decker. The latter is former GS31, bought by Seth early in 1965 for spares and sold for scrap in December 1966. Of the two RTs, the one on the left is RT759, bought in March 1964, which has suffered roof damage. Despite a scrap RTL having been bought to provide new roof parts, this was never done, and the bus was eventually scrapped. The other RT is former RT2621, bought by Seth in May 1964 two months after withdrawal by London Transport and still in use at this time. The coach on the left had one of Harrington's famous 'tail fin' bodies. A fierce Alsatian guarding the yard prevented me getting further details of it!

An oddity seen at Earl's Court for the gathering of the 'faithful' to see American evangelist Billy Graham on 18/6/66 is BSD441, a 1949 Weymann-bodied AEC Regent III lowbridge 53-seater which had been ordered by Scottish Bus Group fleet Western SMT but diverted to York Brothers of Northampton, who sold it to present operator County of Brentwood in 1965.

Seen in Nottingham on 26/6/66, ORR938 is a former Barton BTS1, originally a 39-seat dual-purpose vehicle with Barton's own bodywork built in 1952. It is now a staff bus for Hoveringham Construction.

Another contractor's staff bus seen n Nottingham that day is RN8639, a pre-war Leyland Titan TD4 which had been rebodied in 1949 and originally owned by Ribble.

An independent stage-carriage operator which served the Northamptonshire town of Kettering was Royal Blue of Pytchley, whose 1950 Duple Vista-bodied Bedford OB GDL75 is seen outside the town hall on 19/6/66. It had been new to Southern Vectis on the Isle of Wight.

Billy Graham's 'final' at Wembley Stadium on 2/7/66 has brought hundreds of buses and coaches, of which one of the most unusual is ECX423, a Northern Coachbuilders-bodied AEC Regent III that had been new in 1948 as Huddersfield Corporation No.223, and is now in the fleet of independent operator Pond's Coaches of Nazeing.

A trip to Derby on 3/7/66 finds this unusual-looking Daimler, Tailby & George ('Blue Bus') of Willington working their stage-carriage service to Burton-on-Trent in Derby Bus Station. Built in 1953 with Willowbrook 61-seat highbridge bodywork, it has a rare Daimler CD650 chassis, hence the extraordinarily wide radiator grille.

Hundreds more coaches are at Wembley for the first World Cup match to be held there, on 11/7/66. One of them is GPC58C, a 1965 Bedford VAL14 with Plaxton Panorama 51-seat coachwork belonging to Safeguard of Guildford. It still bears the livery of Cooke of Staughton, whose fleet they had recently taken over.

An unusual, and well-known, independent coach often seen in Central London at this period is Osterley Coaches 2088HX, a Commer Avenger IV with Yeates 'Europa' 41-seat bodywork new in 1960. It is seen at Parliament Square on 15/7/66.

Parked for some reason in my workplace, in County Hall's forecourt on 22/7/66, is JAP103D, a brand new Duple 'Viscount'-bodied Ford Thames R192 45-seater, and the newest coach in the fleet of South East London independent Lewis of Greenwich.

Seen on 23/7/66 at Wembley for another World Cup match, 108DMV, a 1955 Burlingham Seagull-bodied AEC Reliance, is now one of the oldest coaches in the fleet of Valliant of Ealing.

An OTC trip to various operators in Gloucestershire on 24/7/66 finds us at the depot of Warner of Tewkesbury, where ex-London Transport RT242 (HLW229) accompanies ex-Bradford Corporation Roberts-bodied Daimler CVD6 FKY578. The RT had been acquired in early 1959, painted green and fitted with platform doors – it lasted with Warner's until late 1972, having therefore been with them longer than it had been with LT.

Just acquired by Warner's is FCH22, a 1954 Weymann-bodied Leyland Tiger Cub PSUC1/1T 44-seat saloon, which had been new to Trent Motor Traction.

A rather exotic new acquisition by the same fleet is EPG179B, a Dennis Loline III demonstrator, with Northern Counties 76-seat forward-entrance bodywork. It had been exhibited at the 1964 Commercial Motor Show.

Another operator we visited that day was Talbot of Moreton-in-Marsh. Many of their vehicles were used to take workers to and from local factories. One of the more unusual is FAC651C, a 1958 Mulliner-bodied Bedford SB 38-seater which had been new to the RAF and only received a civilian registration when bought by Talbot in 1965.

Talbot also operated schools contracts, and JUO562 is one of the double-deckers used on them. This was new to Devon General as their DR562 in 1948 and is a Weymann-bodied AEC Regent III with highbridge 56-seat bodywork.

Recently acquired by Talbot for the same purpose and in splendid condition is GCD361, a former Southdown 1938 Leyland Titan TD5 54-seater rebodied by Northern Counties in 1949.

Well-known Bournemouth independent operator Shamrock & Rambler Coaches had just been taken over by the Transport Holding Company when their 1963 Duple 'Alpine'-bodied AEC Reliance was seen at Victoria Coach Station working on hire to Royal Blue on 5/8/66.

An elderly rarity seen at Victoria the same day is KYK696, a 1949 Dennis Lancet J3 with full-fronted Duple 37-seat coachwork, belonging to Pocknell's Viola Coaches of Dulwich.

Midland Red's self-built buses rarely saw further use with other operators after withdrawal, but one that did is their former No.3236 (JHA836) which is an S8 with MCCW 44-seat bodywork new in 1948. It is operating for Hulley of Baslow when seen in Chesterfield on 14/8/66.

Another ex-BET vehicle seen with Hulley's on the same occasion is DHE348, a Leyland Royal Tiger PSU1/9 with Brush 43-seat bodywork new to Yorkshire Traction in 1951.

On that day, I was on an OTC tour visiting various operators in South Yorkshire. One of these was Booth & Fisher of Halfway, near Sheffield. This stage-carriage operator had a varied and fascinating fleet, an example of which is CEX491, one of several little Albion Nimbuses in their fleet. This one has Willowbrook 31-seat bodywork and was new in 1959 to Great Yarmouth Corporation, who had sold it to them in 1964.

There were several elderly Bedford OBs in Booth & Fisher's fleet, too. This one, LRB750, was new in 1948 and has very rare Barnaby bodywork. It appears to have lost its offside headlight!

Similarly bereft of its offside headlight, KGY270 is out of use and is a Mulliner-bodied OB 30-seater that had been new in 1949 as a school bus for the London County Council.

This Bedford OB, HUO680, was new to Western National in 1948 and has Beadle 29-seat coachwork.

Yet another OB in Booth & Fisher's fleet is MNU82, one of six supplied to them in 1948 with extremely rare Allsop 29-seat bodies.

Booth & Fisher were still buying new buses in 1966: MNU387D has recently been delivered and is a Ford Thames R226 with Strachans 51-seat dual-purpose bodywork.

URA601 is a Duple Midland 44-seat Leyland Royal Tiger PSU1/13 new to the operator in 1953.

New to Booth & Fisher the following year, 1954, WRA12 is one of two Park Royal-bodied AEC Monocoach 45-seaters in their fleet. By 1966, this was quite a rare type.

Not many Bristol SC4LKs saw further use with independent fleets after sale by Tilling Group companies. With standard ECW 35-seat bodywork, 612JPU was new in 1958 and is one of two acquired by Booth & Fisher from Eastern National in 1964.

Seen at an M1 service station on our way back from South Yorkshire, DJV501C is an ex-Ministry of Supply forces' transport Bedford SB with Mulliner 38-seat bodywork acquired for staff transport by Ross Services in 1965. Note the nasty denting to its nearside front.

On 18/8/66, OHE6 is a Yorkshire-registered 1957 Plaxton-bodied Bedford SBG 41-seater recently acquired by Kap's Coaches of Waterloo, seen parked in Frazier Street.

On 21/8/66, 1961 Duple Midland-bodied 42-seat Ford Thames school bus 707BLU has brought a party of children for a day trip to Hastings. It belongs to the St Maria of Ravensbrook Roman Catholic School, Eltham.

Next day, 22/8/66, 461YMG is one of at least three Valliant of Ealing coaches that have brought day trippers to Brighton. It is a Duple Midland 'Donnington'-bodied AEC Reliance 40-seater new in 1960.

A visit to Eastbourne on 24/8/66 finds HCD447, a 1946 ex-Southdown Leyland Tiger PS1 with ECW 31-seat dual-purpose coachwork, in use by the Council's Welfare Department for the transport of the elderly. Looked after at Eastbourne Corporation's depot, it is named after one of the town's famous personalities, Polly Zelinger.

Another old BET coach in use for charitable purposes on the south coast is KKK852, used by Toc H for the transport of spastics. It is a former Maidstone & District 1949 AEC Regal III with full-fronted Harrington 32-seat coachwork, seen at Worthing Pier on 25/8/66.

Seen in Guildford outside Aldershot & District's depot on 26/8/66 is 5389PL, a Duple Midland 45-seat AEC Reliance, new in 1962 to the well-known independent operator in the town, Safeguard.

A lesser-known independent stage-carriage operator which served Guildford was Brown Motors of Forest Green, whose 3255PJ, a Bedford VAS1 with Willowbrook 31-seat bodywork, also new in 1962, is seen at one of the town's two bus stations.

Back in Hastings, where I was on holiday for the last two weeks of August 1966, Valliant of Ealing 1957 Plaxton-bodied AEC Reliance VUP441 accompanies Windsorian Duple Super Vega-bodied Bedford SB at the Fish Market on 28/8/66.

A small stage-carriage operator which served Hastings at this period was Dengate & Son of Beckley, whose 1948 Duple Vista-bodied Bedford OB No.35 (JXP453) sets off from Warrior Square for home on 29/8/66.

Back in London, Plaxton-bodied Seddon 41-seater SWB200, built in 1953, belongs to Watts' Prospect Coaches of Lye, and is an oddity amongst more mundane coaches at Wembley for a Speedway event on 3/9/66.

Seen in Southend on 17/9/66, ERR601 is a 1938 Bristol L5G with post-war Burlingham 35-seat bodywork now used by CJB Contractors for staff transport.

A real gem in Southend's Kursaal coach park the same day is KAR20C, a 1965 Morris 16-seater with coachwork built by its operator, Stocker of St Margaret's, Hertfordshire.

At the Earls Court Commercial Motor Show on 24//9/66 is this Ford Thames R192 coach, with the latest style of Duple 'Viceroy' 45-seat coachwork. As yet unregistered, it is destined for the fleet of Golden Miller Coaches, Feltham.

Also at the show is CWK641C, a Daimler Roadliner, rear-engined, with Duple 'Commander' 49-seat coachwork. It is a demonstrator for Daimler that had also appeared at the 1964 show. Not many Roadliners were built. This one later passed to Red House Motor Services of Coventry.

At London's Heathrow Airport a number of coaches were operated by British European Airways to ferry passengers from the terminal buildings to the aeroplanes. These were referred to as 'airside coaches'. During 1964/65, a number of surplus Green Line coach RFs were sold to BEA for this work. One is former RF256 (MLL793), seen here at Heathrow on 24/9/66.

Another 'airside coach' seen on the same occasion is PXE101, an ex-Ministry of Supply Bedford SBO with 8ft 6ins wide Mulliner 38-seat bodywork, which has entrances on both sides to speed up loading.

During 1965, BEA took delivery of ten new Marshall-bodied 50-seat Bedford VAL14s for 'airside' duties. LMG164C is one of them, again with an entrance/exit on each side.

A well-known Lancashire independent stage-carriage operator was Fishwick of Leyland, who naturally favoured Leyland products. Seen in Preston on 8/10/66, their No.10 (MTD514) is an MCCW-bodied Olympic 44-seater new in 1951.

Also in the Fishwick fleet is No.18 (529CTF), a 1957 Leyland Titan PD2/40 with Weymann 'Orion' 58-seat lowbridge bodywork.

One of the only Leyland Atlanteans to have an A-suffix registration, ATB598A, is No.32 in the Fishwick fleet. It has MCCW 73-seat bodywork and was new in 1963.

Lancashire United was the biggest independent fleet in the North West. Seen also in Preston on 8/10/66, their No.127 is a 1963 Guy Arab V with Northern Counties 73-seat bodywork working an express service to Blackpool.

At Blackpool
itself later that day, LRM806 is a 1950 AEC Regal III rebodied later in the 1950s by Plaxton with a 35-seat body, belonging to Brownrigg of Egremont.

Seen in Midland Road, St Pancras on 15/10/66, OLG855 is a very unusual Foden PVRF6 rear-engined coach with Plaxton 41-seat bodywork dating from 1951. It belongs to the Chester chassis builder's works brass band and is kept in immaculate condition. So much so, it lasted with them until 1979 and is preserved today!

Also in very smart condition is DCF418, a 1950 Dennis Lancet J3 with Duple 35-seat coachwork owned by Beeston of Hadleigh, Suffolk. It is parked on the South Bank near Waterloo, also on 15/10/66.

On 16/10/66, an Omnibus Touring Circle trip took me to various independent operators in Buckinghamshire and Bedfordshire. Our first port of call was Red Rover at Aylesbury, whose ex-London Transport Cravens-bodied RT1519 (KGK778) is seen here. There were 120 of these RTs, bodied by Cravens of Sheffield, which were non-standard to the rest of the fleet, notably by being of five-bay construction instead of four. The RT, in common with standard examples in the fleet, has had its roof route number box removed. New in early 1950, it was acquired by Red Rover in 1956 and withdrawn two months after this picture was taken, but it saw more years' service with them than it did in London. The Duple-bodied coach on the right belongs to the associated Keith Coaches fleet.

Another operator visited that day was Todd's Coaches of Whitchurch. SKX27D is their newest vehicle, a Ford Thames R192 with Plaxton 45-seat coachwork that has only recently been delivered.

An older Plaxton-bodied coach in Todds' fleet is 702GKX, a 41-seater Bedford SB3 new in 1959.

Todd's Coaches also own one of the first Bedford VAL14s ever built, which has Plaxton Panorama 51-seat coachwork and was new in 1963. 7KX is also perhaps the shortest registration number borne by a British coach at this period.

A unique vehicle with Buckmaster of Leighton Buzzard is XTC684, one of the first Leyland Atlantean rear-engined double-decker prototypes, new in 1955, but with MCCW 61-seat rear entrance bodywork. Its frontal design is not unlike that of the first Routemasters built at the same period.

At this time, London Transport's Potters Bar bus garage was very much underused, and so half of it was leased to Arlington's, a coach dealer. Seen there on 29/10/66 is GRC219, a 1955 Burlingham Seagull-bodied 41-seat Leyland Tiger Cub PSUC1/2 recently retired by Trent Motor Traction and awaiting a new owner. Today, so many London buses are based at Potters Bar garage that an outstation has had to be found for some of them.

Another ex-Trent Leyland seen that day is Cheek's Elms of Kenton 1952 all-Leyland PD2/12 highbridge 58-seater CRC832, which stands at their depot.

Elms also own FDL297, an ex-Southern Vectis Bristol K5G with standard ECW 55-seat lowbridge bodywork. As is just discernable on its blind, this has been working route 98B, part of which (between Ruislip Station and North Harrow) had been relinquished by London Transport in March 1966.

Next day, 30/10/66, finds brand new Safeguard Willowbrook-bodied Bedford VAM dual-purpose 45-seater LPB238D in one of Guildford's bus stations.

Seen at Waterloo Road coach park on 21/11/66, HCU962 is a 1963 Duple 'Commodore'-bodied Leyland Leopard L2 coach new to Hall Brothers of South Shields and recently sold to Silcox of Pembroke Dock.

Still carrying details of destinations its former owner Sutton's Coaches of Clacton served from Kings Cross coach station, 1951 Duple-bodied Leyland Royal Tiger PSU1/15 41-seater SPU906 has just been acquired by Commins' Cornwallis Coaches of Islington. It stands beside Paradise Gardens in Madras Place, just off Holloway Road, on 9/12/66.

Standing at a wintry Highbury Fields the same day, KLT402D is a brand new Marshall-bodied Bedford SB5, specially adapted to carry wheelchairs for Islington Council's Welfare Department.

At a gloomy Manchester, Lower Mosley Street on 10/12/66, 7587TF is quite a rare sight, being a 1963 Leyland Tiger Cub PSU3 36-footer with Duple Dragonfly 51-seat coachwork, belonging to Fishwick of Leyland. To illustrate the eccentricity of some bus and coach enthusiasts, the person crouching and looking at its underbelly is trying to find its chassis frame number to add to his records of such for Leyland vehicles!

Following the closure of Kings Cross Pentonville Road Coach Station, replacement facilities were found on waste ground in Caledonia Street, between York Way and Caledonian Road. On 7/1/67, Jennings of Clare's 1950 MCCW-bodied Leyland Olympic 40-seater SPU985 is seen there.

At Waterloo Road coach park on 11/1/67 is KBD666D, a Duple Vega Major-bodied Bedford VAL14 belonging to Alec Head Coaches of Northampton.

Similar in style is Grey Green's brand new Duple Viceroy-bodied Bedford VAM NMU552E, which has brought a party of theatregoers to Victoria on 4/2/67.

Commins' Cornwallis Coaches was an operator based in Furlong Road, Islington, just five minutes' or so walk from my home. Here on 5/2/67, their GHR366 is a 1950 ECW-bodied Bristol K5G lowbridge 55-seater recently acquired from Wilts & Dorset for school contracts, seen parked outside their depot with one of their newer Plaxton-bodied Bedford coaches.

At Wembley on 4/3/67, HUJ516E is a brand new Duple Viceroy-bodied Bedford VAM in the fleet of well-known Shropshire independent coach operator Whittle of Highley.

Another well-known West Midlands operator was Don Everall of Wolverhampton, who operated luxury coaches as well as double-deckers for school and industrial contracts. Seen under the trolleybus wires in its hometown on 5/3/67, JP6003 is an ex-Wigan Corporation all-Leyland Titan PD1 lowbridge 53-seater new in 1947.

Another former Tilling Group ECW-bodied Bristol lowbridge 55-seater in non-PSV use is EJB241, a 1948 K6B previously owned by Thames Valley and now used by Hounslow Evangelical Church for Sunday School outings. It is seen at the church on 18/3/67.

Not far away, four early Bedford Vega-bodied Bedford SBs are parked out of use in the yard of Garner's Coaches of Hounslow. XMT329 is nearest to the camera.

Seen on 9/4/67 at the premises of famous Huntingdonshire independent operator Whippet of Hilton, former London Transport lowbridge Weymann-bodied AEC Regent III MXX248 had been RLH48 in LT's fleet. Sold to Whippet in September 1965, it remained with them until 1974 when it was sold for preservation. It remains in preserved state today.

Eastern Belle Coaches of Bow were well-known for keeping half-cab coaches in service well into the mid-1960s. One of these was 1950 AEC Regal LLT561, seen also on 22/4/67 in the Edgware Road after sale to the highways contractor Fitzpatrick & Sons Ltd.

'**Provincial**', **or** Gosport & Fareham as the operator was often known, was an independent stage carriage operator renowned for keeping pre-war vehicles going well into the late 1960s. An example of this is their No.18 (FHO602), an AEC Regent with original Park Royal 56-seat bodywork, seen at their Hoeford depot on 23/4/67. The two single-deckers on the right are pre-war AEC Regals, which were rebodied in the 1950s.

Also rebodied is Provincial's No.72 (HHA84), a wartime utility Guy Arab given a new full-fronted Reading body as well as a Deutz air-cooled engine! It is seen with some of their other double-deckers in Hoeford depot.

Back at Wembley on 29/4/67, Osborne's of Tollesbury, Essex have sent their Park Royal-bodied AEC Bridgemaster 2211MK, a former demonstrator, with a party of spectators.

At the lower end of the scale, 1949 Duple Vista-bodied Bedford OB 29-seater KKN752, belonging to Moody's Coaches of Northfleet, contrasts with a larger and newer Bedford SB with Duple Bella Vega bodywork.

Bearing what would become a rare Weymann 'Topaz II' body, 1965 Bedford VAL14 JNK686C is on hire to Evan Evans tours at the same event.

Heading a procession of Plaxton-bodied coaches, LCY782 is a former Neath & Cardiff Luxury Coaches 1955 Guy Arab LUF with Park Royal 41-seat coachwork now with Stevenage Travel.

This strange-looking little coach, 286CDH, is a Thames Trader with Willowbrook coachwork, belonging to Happy Days Coaches of Wolverhampton.

Another oddity at Wembley that day is MXL329, a 1951 Bedford SB with rare Gurney Nutting bodywork, operated by Bestway Coaches.

HWS940 is an early AEC Regal IV with Alexander bodywork originally belonging to Western SMT, but now in the service of Southgate Coaches.

Seen outside Reading General Station next day, 30/4/67, LJB417E is a brand new Duple Viceroy-bodied Bedford VAM working a dedicated 'Railair' link between the stations here and Heathrow Airport.

Seen in Brighton on 7/5/67, JUP609 is a Bedford OB with Duple Vista 29-seat coachwork operated by Polegate Motors.

Seen near Crawley on the same day, FJN206 is a former Westcliffe-On-Sea and Eastern National all-Leyland PD2/12 lowbridge 53-seater, new in 1952 and originally used on route 251 between Wood Green and Southend. It is now owned by Super of Upminster and used for driver training.

At Wembley on 13/5/67, DWG944 is a very rare Foden PVRF6 coach with Plaxton 41-seat coachwork. Originally built for a Scottish operator in 1951, this rear-engined vehicle is now owned by its manufacturer's welfare department.

Also at Wembley that day, Wallace Arnold 1960 Plaxton 'Consort'-bodied AEC Reliance 41-seater 5628UB is in its last season with the operator, and accompanies 8334U, another Reliance with an earlier version of the same bodywork, new to them in 1958 but sold to D. Hughes in 1965.

Quite an unusual combination of chassis and body is represented by Happiways of Rochdale's VTC589D, a 1966 Albion Victor with Duple Firefly bodywork. It was one of the last Albion Victors built.

Seen parked in Midland Road, St Pancras on 21/5/67, RDU905 is a mid-1950s Burlingham Seagull-bodied AEC Reliance belonging to Camm's Coaches of Nottingham.

Unfortunately, Harrington's of Hove ceased coach production early in 1966. One of their last vehicles was JHV495D, a 51-seat Leyland Leopard built for Grey Green. It is seen also on 21/5/67 at the Watford Gap service station on the M1 whilst taking me on an OTC trip to Sheffield.

At Sheffield itself on 21/5/67 is LFM314, an early post-war Leyland Tiger which had been new to Crosville, and is now working for building contractor Shand.

Another former Tilling Group vehicle in use as a contractor's staff bus is FJN169, a 39-seat ECW-bodied Bristol LS6G new in 1953 to Westcliffe-on-Sea, which had been taken over by Eastern National in 1955 and ended its days with them as their No.314. It is seen passing Kilburn Station on 25/5/67.

At a time when London Transport were rapidly withdrawing their RTL-class Leyland Titan PD buses, examples of this type they had sold off in earlier years could be seen with independent operators in London. Two examples are seen here on Victoria Embankment in the ownership of H&C Coaches, Garston on 3/6/67. The leading bus is former RTL443 (KLB630) which they had bought in August 1966. It remained with them until the end of 1969.

A London-based luxury coach tour operator was Glenton Tours. Their 1961 Plaxton-bodied AEC Reliance 79BLT stands on Eccleston Bridge, Victoria on the evening of 10/6/67. The coach is in its last season of service for Glenton. This location is most well-known for scenes of Green Line coaches; I must have taken dozens of photographs here in the 1960s and 1970s!

Barton of Chilwell still had plenty of unusual vehicles when I visited their headquarters depot again on an OTC tour on 11/6/67. One of the oldest vehicles present that day was HL8613, a pre-war Roe-bodied Leyland TD Titan which had been new to Yorkshire independent operator West Riding. Now out of service, it appears to have been adapted for use as a tree-lopper.

Another old Barton vehicle converted to non-passenger use is this BTS dual-purpose single-decker, now in use as a towing wagon.

Typifying Barton's more modern vehicles is their No.861, a Dennis Loline III new in 1960, with special low-height Northern Counties full-fronted 68-seat bodywork.

A more conventional vehicle in Barton's fleet is No.855, an all-Leyland Titan PD1 lowbridge 53-seater new to Western Welsh in 1947 and sold to Barton in 1960.

A new acquisition in Barton's fleet is No.1087, also a lowbridge 53-seater but an AEC Regent III with Park Royal bodywork new in 1954 to Nottingham City Transport.

An AEC Regent of different pedigree working for Barton is their No.883, a former London Transport Cravens-bodied RT new in 1949. It was one of two acquired with the business of Cream Bus Services of Stamford in 1961. New as LT's RT1472 and sold in 1956, it has now just been withdrawn by Barton and will be sold for scrap two months after this picture was taken.

A more recent Barton AEC is Regent V No.850, one of five with special low-height 70-seat bodies built by Northern Counties in 1960.

With a type of ECW bodywork more usually associated with early post-war Bristol K types, Barton No.940 is a 53-seat lowbridge Leyland Titan PD1A new in 1947 and one of two acquired from Crosville in 1961.

Barton No.915 is another 1947 Leyland Titan, in this case a PD1 with Weymann 53-seat lowbridge bodywork. It is one of three acquired from Chesterfield Corporation in 1961.

Barton had a number of unusual single-deckers and coaches too. One of these is No.967, a 1963 Bedford VAL14 twin-steerer, with Yeates dual-purpose, dual-entrance 36ft-long bodywork on which 56 passengers could be squeezed! Of particular note are the large 'IN' and 'OUT' signs by each door. At this period, this mode of loading and unloading was quite unusual.

It was also unusual for Duple Super Vega coach bodies to be fitted out for dual-purpose operation, but Barton's No.910, a 1961 Bedford SB1 41-seater is so equipped.

A more conventional Barton coach is No.777, one of five Alexander-bodied AEC Reliance 37-seaters new in 1958. It is seen in Nottingham working a Barton express service to Leicester.

On the same occasion, Barton No.506, one of their ornate Duple-bodied Leyland Titan PD1 55-seaters new in 1948 is still going strong, and accompanies a 1967 Bristol RE/ECW coach working United Counties' motorway express service to London.

In Nottingham, Barton 731 is, for once, a conventional vehicle that had been new to the operator! It is an all-Leyland PD2/12 with 58-seat highbridge bodywork, one of two that were new to them in 1953. It accompanies one of fellow-independent operator W. Gash of Newark's double-deckers in Huntingdon Street Bus Station.

The W. Gash & Sons' vehicle seen in the previous picture, their No.DD1 (KAL578), one of four Daimler CVD6's new in 1948 and given new Massey 61-seat bodies between 1958 and 1962, sets off for its home town, Newark.

A visit to Staffordshire independent stage-carriage operator Harper of Heath Hayes on 18/6/67 finds KRE849 at their depot. This is an early post-war Guy Arab with very ornate Burlingham bodywork.

With a group of RT-type double-deckers in the background, Harper of Heath Hayes' No.5 (KOH80) is an AEC Regal III with Burlingham 33-seat coachwork, new in 1950.

Amongst several London Transport-style vehicles with Harper's, their No.8 (BDJ802) is actually an RT which has Park Royal bodywork identical externally to LT examples. It was new to St Helen's Corporation in 1952. They had twenty-five of these in 1952, in addition to a previous fifteen built in 1950. These forty RTs were the only ones identical to London's that were new to a fleet outside the capital.

Conversely, non-standard Cravens-bodied RT KGK729 was new to London Transport as their RT1470 in 1949, and acquired by Harper's in January 1957. Withdrawn by them in March 1968, it accompanies another elderly AEC Regal III, No.42 (TRE251)

Another early post-war half-cab coach in Harper's fleet is No.47 (TRF405), a Leyland Tiger PS2 new in 1950.

Another Staffordshire independent stage-carriage operator at this period was Stonier of Goldenhill. On 24/6/67, their No.5 (ERN689) seen in Longton is a 1951 all-Leyland 44-seat Royal Tiger that had been new to Ribble.

Beresford's was another independent stage carriage operator in Staffordshire that had a fascinating array of buses and coaches. One is their No.40 (XMW706), a Weymann-bodied Leyland Atlantean with 61 coach seats. It had been new to Silver Star of Porton Down in 1961, and was acquired via Super of Upminster in April 1967. It is also seen in Longton. Unfortunately, this splendid vehicle was destroyed by fire in 1970.

Leaving Longton Bus Station on the same day is Beresford's No.50 (DDV425), a Weymann Orion-bodied AEC Regent 56-seater that had been new to Devon General in 1939 and rebuilt and rebodied in 1954. It was acquired by Beresford's in 1963.

Another Beresford's vehicle is No. 31 (CRJ364), one of ninety Metro-Cammell-bodied Daimler CVG6s that had been new to Salford City Transport in 1950, seen arriving at Longton Bus Station. It was acquired in November 1965.

Prior to travelling to this area, I had been told that Beresford's depot at the village of Cheddleton had very many ancient vehicles dumped out of use, and therefore I made sure to travel to there! I was not disappointed, though the first vehicle to greet me there, DBN352, one of a hundred all-Leyland 58-seat highbridge PD2/4s new to Bolton Corporation in 1948/49, was quite ordinary compared to many others on the premises. It had become No.36 in Beresford's fleet in October 1966.

The first example of an oddity at Beresford's premises is STC488, an early AEC Regal IV with Whitson bodywork, apparently acquired for spares only.

The tales I had heard were true, as shown by the remains of two pre-war double-deckers at Cheddleton! Nearest the camera is what had been Bradford Corporation No.402.

Amongst more mouldering relics in Beresford's yard, No.27 (JX6894), a former Halifax Corporation Roe-bodied AEC Regent dating from 1938, is nearest the camera. It was acquired in 1957 and withdrawn two years later.

A pre-war Leyland Lion is also present, HE5224 which had been No.9 in Beresford's fleet. With Leyland 30-seat bodywork, it had been new to Yorkshire Traction as their No. 340. It was acquired by Beresford's in 1940 and withdrawn as long ago as 1949.

Single-decker KWJ103 originated with Sheffield City Transport and had latterly been used by contractor McAlpine before being acquired by Beresford's for spares. It is a Leyland Tiger PS1 with very rare Cawood 34-seat bodywork, new in 1949, and also acquired by Beresford's for spares only.

GBU729 is an early Leyland Royal Tiger coach with Bellhouse-Hartwell coachwork that has been put out to grass with some of Beresford's lorries after being acquired for spares.

EN8252 is another elderly double-decker slowly falling apart at Beresford's premises. It is a Leyland Titan TD7 with Northern Counties 56-seat bodywork new to Bury Corporation as their No.88 in 1940, acquired in 1953 but withdrawn the following year.

Two more recent double-deckers out of use at Beresford's premises are DBR43, a Daimler CVG5 with Roe 58-seat bodywork new to Sunderland Corporation only in 1953 and acquired for spares, and No.34 (GTD487), a Leyland Titan PD1 with Alexander 56-seat bodywork new in 1946 to Accrington Corporation. This was acquired in October 1959 and withdrawn at the end of 1964.

Also out of action at Beresford's depot after acquisition for spares is HG9416, an all-Leyland Titan PD2/3 56-seater new to Burnley, Colne & Nelson Joint Transport Committee in 1947. It accompanies another of the ex-Salford Daimlers, No.34 (FRJ504), which had been acquired in September 1966.

SFC431 is an AEC Regent III with Weymann 56-seat bodywork new in 1951 acquired from City of Oxford Motor Services in July 1966, and apparently being prepared for service with Beresford's.

Another all-Leyland Titan at Beresford's, No. 38 (HTF823), a 1947 PD2/1 56-seater, came from Accrington Corporation in November 1960 and has apparently been cannibalised for spare body parts following withdrawal in October 1963.

Next to the former Accrington Titan, Beresford's No.43 (BRJ939) appears to have had a nasty accident with a low bridge. It is an MCCW-bodied PD1 54-seater that was new to Salford City Transport in 1947, acquired in 1962 and withdrawn two years later.

Two more pre-war double-deckers dumped at Cheddleton are former Salford Corporation Nos 55 & 57 (RJ6828 and RJ6830).

Still in service with Beresford's is their No.32 (CRJ357), another ex-Salford City 54-seat MCCW-bodied Daimler CVG6 new in 1950 and acquired in February 1966.

Whether ex-Devon General Weymann-rebodied 1939 AEC Regent DDV423 was deroofed in a low bridge accident, or purposefully cut down for tree-lopping purposes, history does not relate! At any rate, it was not operated by Beresford's.

DOD489 is another ex-Devon General Weymann-rebodied 1939 AEC Regent that is in service with Beresford's. It was purchased in February 1964 and accompanies their Commer-Beadle integral 41-seat coach No.26 (26LHX), new in 1957 and acquired in March 1965. Beresford's varied fleet continued to operate until the autumn of 1987.

Passing Beresford's premises is a vehicle with another of the area's independent stage carriage operators, ex-London Transport RT4420 (NXP774) which has been with Procter of Hanley since May 1964. It was withdrawn in January 1963 by LT and is unusual in having its roof route number box retained in use by its new operator.

Yet another independent operator in the area is Turner of Brown Edge. Their KRE866B, a Leyland Titan PD2 with Massey forward-entrance bodywork new in 1964, is seen arriving at Hanley Bus Station, also on 24/6/67.

At the same location, RRR104 is a 1955 Leyland Titan PD2/20 with Weymann 55-seat lowbridge bodywork, recently acquired by Stonier of Goldenhill.

Next day, 25/6/67 Leighton Coaches' Duple Firefly-bodied Bedford SB VDY213 has taken me on an enthusiasts' tour to various operators in Bedfordshire, and is seen at Luton United Counties depot.

An independent operator we visited that day was Wesley of Stoke Goldington. Their DJY965 is a very unusual vehicle for the area, a Crossley DD42/7 with Manchester-style bodywork new in 1948 as Plymouth Corporation No.335.

A newer double-decker with Wesley's is PDV724, an ex-Devon General AEC Regent III with 'tin-front' Weymann Orion bodywork.

Wesley's evidently favoured Commer coaches, as all three of these, Duple-bodied 411BYR and SOX859 and Plaxton-bodied RLJ855 are Commer 'Avengers' dating from the mid-1950s until 1961.

Although Birch Brothers were based in Kentish Town, London and operated limited-stop services from Kings Cross to Bedfordshire and north Hertfordshire, they also had stage carriage services beyond the London Transport area. Here their K41, a 1958 Park Royal-bodied AEC Reliance, is seen working their route 211 at Bedford Bus Station.

East London independent operator Galleon Tours is the owner of this smart Plaxton-bodied AEC Reliance, SAN258, seen at one of the service stations on the M1 on 2/7/67.

New to Yelloway of Rochdale for the 1967 summer season, HDK45E is a Plaxton Panorama-bodied Bedford VAL14, seen on their Cambridge service in Derby Bus Station, also on 2/7/67.

Seen at Stratford Broadway on 13/8/67, LYD134 is an early post-war AEC Regal III with full-fronted coachwork now in use as a staff bus for building contractor Fitzpatrick.

Essex Independent operator Osborne's of Tollesbury had several ex-London Transport RF and RT class buses. Their No.42, former RF211, is seen at Colchester Bus Station on 3/9/67. It was one of a number of surplus Green Line RFs sold by LT in the mid-1960s.

Bedford OBs were still going strong at this period. At a very wet Clacton the same day, Mulley of Ixworth's 1948 Duple Vista-bodied CCF649 is one of two in the seafront coach park.

As if sheltering from the rain, Sutton's of Clacton's Duple-bodied Leyland Royal Tiger VVW531 and AEC Reliance 6801HK are seen in their depot and coach station in this Essex seaside town.

A somewhat surprising find on our enthusiasts' tour that day was this group of thirteen former East Kent all-Leyland PD1s dating from 1947, in use with a contractor near Dovercourt and painted in yellow livery. CJG967 is nearest to the camera.

For an Omnibus Touring Circle weekend trip to operators in Cheshire and Lancashire, Birch Brothers' splendid 1964 Harrington Cavalier-bodied AEC Reliance K27 was our mode of transport. We travelled from London to Altrincham, where the coach is seen outside our hotel on 9/9/67.

Britain's largest independent bus and coach operator in the 1960s was Lancashire United Transport. Here in Wigan on 10/9/67 is their 1963 Plaxton-bodied AEC Reliance 50-seater No.144. At this period, Plaxton bus bodies were a rarity, unlike in more recent years when they produced bodies for thousands of Dennis Darts!

A visit to Lancashire United's Atherton depot on the same day sees their No.528, a rare Atkinson Alpha PM745H with Roe 44-seat body work which was new in 1954 contrasting with the Birch Brothers coach which took us there.

With distinctive Northern Counties 57-seat bodywork, Lancashire United No.533 is one of ten Guy Arab IVs also delivered in 1954.

Illustrating how Bristol products could now be sold new to operators other than those within the Tilling Group, even including independent fleets, LUT No.246 is a brand new Bristol RE with Plaxton dual-entrance bodywork.

One of the nearest independent operators to my home was Cream Coaches of Islington. Here on the morning of 13/9/67, their 1961 Duple Super Vega-bodied Bedford SB 1193AR is one of two outside their offices at Islington, Angel.

Seen in Oxford Bus Station on 1/10/67, TGJ488 is a Commer-Beadle integral coach new to Timpson's of Catford in 1957, and now working for Charlton-on-Otmoor Services.

An oddity seen at Parliament Square on 6/10/67 is former Western Welsh Harrington-bodied Albion Nimbus 30-seater TUH24, new in 1960 and now owned as staff transport by Office Cleaning Services Ltd.

Seen beneath a wonderful web of trolleybus wires in Bradford on 7/10/67, BCK427 is 1947 ex-Ribble Burlingham-bodied Leyland Titan PD2 now operated by Samuel Ledgard of Leeds. A Bradford Corporation AEC Regent V follows.

Samuel Ledgard also had a large fleet of ex-London Transport RTs. One of them, KGK687, had been RT1218 which Ledgard's had bought in 1963. Here it is seen arriving at their Bradford terminus. Sadly, however, just a week after this picture was taken, Ledgard's long-established bus and coach firm was taken over by Tilling Group operator West Yorkshire, and all of their interesting old vehicles were withdrawn.

Wallace Arnold was another well-known Yorkshire independent operator. Best known for its touring coaches, it also operated a number of stage-carriage services under the names of its subsidiaries, one of which was the Farsley Omnibus Company. Also seen in Bradford on 7/10/67 is their MUM458, a 1950 Daimler CVD6SD with 1957 Roe 61-seat highbridge bodywork.

The biggest of all independent bus operators in Yorkshire was West Riding. This fleet was well-known for its faith in the ill-fated Guy Wulfrunian double-deckers, and had all but a handful of the 140-odd built. This one, their No.1021, is one of a batch of thirty built in 1965 with Roe 75-seat front-entrance bodywork. This high seating capacity was achieved partly by having the staircase on the nearside, rather than the offside as was usual for buses of this configuration. It is seen leaving Bradford city centre for Wakefield.

One of the former Silver Star Harrington-bodied Leyland Tiger Cubs, NMW340 dating from 1956, has now been sold to Elms of Kenton, and is seen in Watford with a school party on 21/10/67.

Typical of many small independent operators, Kirby's Luxury Coaches was based in Watford and standardised on Duple-bodied Bedfords. Bella Vega-bodied SB 4007AW is one of three seen in their depot, also on 21/10/67.

Another local operator in Watford at this period is Knightswood Coaches, whose Plaxton Panorama-bodied Bedford VAM XAR819E is the latest addition to their fleet.

The new addition to Knightswood's fleet in 1966 was Plaxton Panorama-bodied Bedford VAL14 NJH814D.

In contrast to Knightswood's modern Plaxton-bodied coaches seen above, the fleet also had ex-London Transport RT445 (HLX262) for school contracts. Sold in 1963 to Ronsway of Hemel Hempstead, it was acquired three years later by Knightswood and withdrawn early in 1969.

Until the sale of ex-London Transport Routemasters to provincial bus operators began in the mid-1980s, the last trip I did to such fleets was an Omnibus Touring Circle visit to the Nottingham area on 28/4/68. Here in Nottingham itself that day, Barton 1948 Duple 55-seat Lowbridge Leyland Titan PD1 No.469 is still in service, having achieved twenty years with its original operator.

At Barton's Ilkeston depot, No.847 is an all-Leyland highbridge 56-seater that had been new to Leicester City in 1946, and acquired by them in 1959.

My reason for attending this trip was to photograph the ex-London RTLs that comprised most of Ilkeston's allocation, having arrived between 1965 and 1968. Former RTL1482 (OLD591) is now Barton No.1032. The bus behind it is their lone RTW, ex-RTW341 (KXW441) numbered 1035 by Barton, which even in this view displays its extra six inches' width. Both were acquired by them in December 1965, lasting until April and September 1971 respectively.

An oddity amongst the standard Park Royal or Weymann-bodied RTLs acquired by Barton No.1086, former RTL810, one of the 450 that had MCCW bodies. It was acquired by Barton in April 1967 and withdrawn in May 1970.

ABOUT THE AUTHOR

I was born at the end of 1947, just five days before the 'Big Four' railway companies, and many bus companies – including London Transport – were nationalised by Clement Attlee's Labour government.

Like most young lads born in the early post-war years, I soon developed a passionate interest in railways, the myriad steam engines still running on Britain's railways in those days in particular. However, because my home in Canonbury Avenue, Islington was just a few minutes' walk from North London's last two tram routes, the 33 in Essex Road and the 35 in Holloway Road and Upper Street, my parents often took me on these for outings to the South Bank, particularly to the Festival of Britain which was held there in the last summer they ran, in 1951. Moreover, my father worked at the GPO's West Central District Office in Holborn and often travelled to and from work on the 35 tram. As a result, I knew many of the tram crews, who would let me stand by the driver at the front of the trams as they travelled through the Kingsway Tram Subway. This was an unforgettable experience for a four-year-old! In addition, my home was in the heart of North London's trolleybus system, with route 611 actually passing my home, and one of the busiest and most complicated trolleybus junctions in the world – Holloway, Nag's Head – a short ride away along Holloway Road. Here, the trolleybuses overhead almost blotted out the sky! Thus from a very early age, I developed an interest in buses and trolleybuses which was equal to my interest in railways, and I have retained both until the present day.

I was educated at my local Highbury County Grammar School, and later at Kingsway College, by coincidence a stone's throw from the old tram subway. I was first bought a camera for my 14th birthday at the end of 1961, which was immediately put to good use photographing the last London trolleybuses in North West London on their very snowy last day a week later. Three years later, I started work as an administrator for the old London County Council at County Hall, by coincidence adjacent to the former Festival of Britain site. I travelled to and from work on bus routes 171 or 172, which had replaced the 33 and 35 trams mentioned above.

By now, my interest in buses and trolleybuses had expanded to include those of other operators, and I travelled throughout England and Wales between 1961 and 1968 in pursuit of them, being able to afford to travel further afield after starting work. I also bought a colour cine-camera in 1965, with which I was able to capture what is now very rare footage of long-lost buses, trolleybuses and steam locomotives. Where the latter are concerned, I was one of the initial purchasers of the unique British Railways 'Pacific' locomotive 71000 *Duke of Gloucester*, which was the last ever passenger express engine built for use in Britain. Other preservationists laughed at our group which had purchased what in effect was a cannibalised hulk from Barry scrapyard at the end of 1973, but they laughed on the other side of their faces when, after extensive and innovative rebuilding, it steamed again in 1986. It has since become one of the best-known and loved preserved British locomotives, often returning to the main lines.

Although I spent thirty-five years in local government administration, with the LCC's successor, the Greater London Council, then Haringey Council and finally literally back on my old doorstep, with Islington Council, I also took a break from office drudgery in 1974/5 and actually worked on the buses as a conductor at London Transport's Clapton Garage, on local routes 22, 38 and 253. Working on the latter, a former tram and trolleybus route, in particular was an unforgettable experience. I was recommended for promotion as an inspector, but rightly thought that taking such a job with the surname Blake was unwise in view of the then-current character of the same name and occupation in the *On The Buses* TV series and films, and so declined the offer and returned to County Hall!

By this time, I had begun to have my transport photographs published in various books and magazines featuring buses. I had also started off the North London Transport Society, which catered for enthusiasts interested in the subject. In conjunction with this group, I have also compiled and published a number of books since 1977, featuring many of the 100,000 or so transport photographs I have taken over the years.

Also through the North London Transport Society, I became involved in setting up and organising various events for transport enthusiasts in 1980, notably the North Weald Bus Rally which the group took over in 1984, and which raised thousands of pounds for charity until it was discontinued in 2016. The group's smaller events are still going strong today.

In addition to my interest in public transport, I also have an interest in the popular music of the late 1950s and early 1960s, in particular that of the eccentric independent record producer, songwriter and manager Joe Meek. In Joe's tiny studio above a shop in Holloway Road (not far from the famous trolleybus junction) he wrote and produced *Telstar* by The Tornados, which became the first British pop record to make No.1 in America, at the end of 1962, long before The Beatles had even been heard of over there! When Joe died in February 1967, I set up an Appreciation Society for his music, which is still going strong today. His music has a very distinctive sound.

I also enjoy a pint or two (and usually more) of real ale. I have two grown-up daughters, Margaret and Felicity, and four grandchildren, Gracie, Freddie, Oscar and Ava, at the time of writing. I still live in North London, having moved to my present home in Palmers Green in 1982.